D0712073

THE
Sin-eater

Also by Thomas Lynch

THE
Sin-eater

——

A BREVIARY

THOMAS LYNCH

WITH PHOTOGRAPHS BY MICHAEL LYNCH

PARACLETE PRESS
BREWSTER, MASSACHUSETTS

The Sin-eater: A Breviary
Copyright © 2011 by Thomas Lynch

ISBN 978-1-55725-872-4

Library of Congress Cataloging-in-Publication Data
Lynch, Thomas, 1948-
  The sin-eater : a breviary / Thomas Lynch ; with photographs by Michael
Lynch.
    p. cm.
  Includes bibliographical references.
  ISBN 978-1-55725-872-4
  I. Title.
  PS3562.Y437S46 2011
  811'.54–dc22   2011010839

10 9 8 7 6 5 4 3 2 1

Published by Paraclete Press
Brewster, Massachusetts
www.paracletepress.com
Printed in the United States of America

Contents

THIS BOOK IS FOR

J.J. McMahon
and in memory of Sonny Carmody

KITCHEN SHRINE MOVEEN

Introit

ARGYLE, the sin-eater, came into being in the hard winter of 1984. My sons were watching a swashbuckler on T.V.— *The Master of Ballantrae*—based on Robert Louis Stevenson's novel about Scots brothers and their imbroglios. I was dozing in the wingback after a long day at the funeral home, waking at intervals too spaced to follow the narrative arc.

But one scene I half wakened to—the gauzy edges of memory still give way—involved a corpse laid out on a board in front of a stone tower house, kinsmen and neighbors gathered round in the grey, sodden moment. Whereupon a figure of plain force, part pirate, part panhandler, dressed in tatters, unshaven and wild-eyed, assumed what seemed a liturgical stance over the body, swilled beer from a wooden bowl, and tore at a heel of bread with his teeth. Wiping his face on one arm, with the other he thrust his open palm at the woman nearest him. She pressed a coin into it spitefully and he took his leave. Everything was grey: the rain and fog, the stone tower, the mourners, the corpse, the countervailing ambivalences between the widow and the horrid man. *Swithering* is the Scots word for it—to be of two minds, in two realities at once: grudging and grateful, faithful and doubtful, broken and beatified—caught between a mirage and an apocalypse. The theater of it was breathtaking, the bolt of drama. I was fully awake. It was over in ten, maybe fifteen seconds.

I knew him at once.

The scene triggered a memory of a paragraph I'd read twelve
years before in mortuary school, from *The History of American
Funeral Directing* by Robert Habenstein and William Lamers. I
have that first edition, by Bulfin Printers of Milwaukee circa
1955.

The paragraph in Chapter III, page 128 at the bottom reads:

A nod should be given to customs that disappeared. Puckle

tells of a curious functionary, a sort of male scapegoat called

the "sin-eater." It was believed in some places that by eating a

loaf of bread and drinking a bowl of beer over a corpse, and

by accepting a six-pence, a man was able to take unto himself

the sins of the deceased, whose ghost thereafter would no

longer wander.

The "Puckle" referenced was Bertram S. Puckle, a British
scholar, whose *Funeral Customs, Their Origin and Development*
would take me another forty years to find and read. But the bit
of cinema and the bit of a book had aligned like tumblers of
a combination lock clicking into place and opening a vault of
language and imagination.

————

I was raised by Irish Catholics. Even as I write that it sounds
a little like "wolves" or some especially feral class of creature.
Not in the nineteenth century, nativist sense of brutish hordes
and apish drunkards, rather in the sense of sure faith and
fierce family loyalties, the pack dynamics of their clannishness,
their vigilance and pride. My parents were grandchildren of
immigrants who had all married within their tribe. They'd sailed
from nineteeth-century poverty into the prospects of North
America, from West Clare and Tipperary, Sligo and Kilkenny, to

Montreal and Ontario, upper and lower Michigan. Graces and
O'Haras, Ryans and Lynches—they brought their version of the
"one true faith," druidic and priest-ridden, punctilious and full
of superstitions, from the boggy parishes of their ancients to the
fertile expanse of middle America. These were people who saw
statues move, truths about the weather in the way a cat warmed
to the fire, omens about coming contentions in a pair of shoes
left up on a table, bad luck in some numbers, good fortune
in others. Odd lights in the nightscape foreshadowed death;
dogs' eyes attracted lightening; the curse of an old spinster
could lay one low. The clergy were to be "given what's going to
them," but otherwise, "not to be tampered with." Priests were
feared and their favor curried—their curses and their blessings
opposing poles of the powerful medicine they were known to
possess. The only moderating influence to this bloodline and
gene pool was provided by my paternal grandmother, a woman
of Dutch extraction, who came from a long line of Daughters
of the American Revolution. She was a temperate, Methodist,
an Eisenhower Republican—she voted for him well into the
1980s—a wonderful cook and seamstress and gardener who
never gossiped or gave any scandal to her family until early
in the so-called roaring twenties, when she was smitten by
and betrothed to marry an Irish Catholic. This was not good
news to her parents and their circle. As was the custom of her
generation, and to appease his priest, she "converted" to what
she would ever after refer to as, "the one true faith?"—the lilt
appended to the end of the declarative easing a foot of doubt
into the door of surety, as if the apostle with a finger in the
wounds of the risen Christ had queried, "My Lord, My God?"
She took a kind of dark glee in explaining the conversion
experience to her grandchildren, to wit: "Ah, the priest
splashed a little water on me and said, 'Geraldine, you were

born a Methodist, raised a Methodist . . . Thanks be to God, now you're Catholic.'" Some weeks after the eventual nuptials, she was out in the backyard, grilling sirloins for my grandfather on the first Friday in Lent, when one of the brother knights from the K. of C. leapt over the back fence to upbraid her for the smell of beef rising over a Catholic household during the holy season. And she listened to your man, nodded and smiled, walked over to the garden hose, splashed water on the grill and said, "You were born cows, raised cows . . . thanks be to God, now you are fish." Then sent the nosey neighbor on his way. "Surely, we are all God's children," she would append to her telling this, "the same but different."

Her telling of this filled me with doubts and wonders, which seem these years since like elements of faith. To be awestruck was better than certainty. And I was smitten at the power of language, which could, in a twinkling, turn cows into fish. It made me hunger for such "authority." It made me less of a Catholic I suppose, variously devout and devoutly lapsed, and yet more catholic somehow—in the way Paul wrote to the Corinthians in the first century after Christ, and John XXIII wrote in the last: a sense that we are all fellow pilgrims in search of a way home.

For all her efforts at temperance, my grandmother became, like many converts, as crazed as the unruly crowd she'd married into for whom everything had meaning beyond the obvious and life was the slow unfolding of metaphors and mysteries the cipher for which lay just beyond our reach. The dead were everywhere and their ghosts inhabited the air and memory and their old haunts, real as ever, if in an only slightly former tense, in constant need of care and appeasement. They were, like the saints they'd been named for, prayed over, prayed to, invoked as protection against all enemies, their names recycled through generations, reassigned to new incarnations.

———

I was named for a dead priest, my father's uncle. Some few years after surviving the Spanish flu epidemic of 1918, he got "the call." ("Vocations follow famine," an Irish bromide holds. No less the flu?) He went to seminary in Detroit and Denver and was ordained in the middle of the Great Depression. We have a photo of his "First Solemn High Mass" on June 10, 1934, at St. John's Church in Jackson, Michigan, a block from the clapboard house he'd grown up in. His father, my great-grandfather, another Thomas Lynch, did not live to get into this photo of women in print dresses and men in straw boaters on a sunny June Sunday between world wars. He had come from the poor townland of Moveen on the West Clare peninsula that forms the upper lip of the gaping mouth of the river Shannon—a treeless sloping plain between the ocean and the estuary, its plots of pasturage divided by hedgerows and intermarriages. He'd come to Michigan for the work available at the huge penitentiary there in Jackson where he painted cellblocks, worked in the laundry, and finished his career as a uniformed guard. He married a Ryan woman, fathered a daughter who taught, a son who got good work with the post office, and now a priest—like hitting the trifecta for a poor Irish "yank," all cushy jobs with reliable pensions.

He never saw Ireland again.

———

In the middle of the retinue of family and parishioners, posed for the photo at the doors to the church around their freshly minted, homegrown priest, is my father, aged ten years, seated next to his father and mother, bored but obedient in his new knee breeches. Because the young priest—he has just going thirty—is sickly but willing, the bishop in Detroit will send him back out west to the bishop in Santa Fe who assigns him to the parish of Our Lady of Guadalupe, in Taos, in hopes that the high, dry air of the Sangre de Christo Mountains might ease his upper respiratory ailments and lengthen his days.

He is going to die just two years later, of pneumonia, at the end of July 1936. The Apache women whose babies he baptized, whose sons he taught to play baseball, whose husbands he preached to, will process his rough-sawn coffin down the mountains from Taos, along the upper reaches of the Rio Grande, through landscapes Georgia O'Keefe will make famous, to the Cathedral in Santa Fe where Archbishop Rudolph Gerken will preside over his requiems, then send his body back to his people, C.O.D., on a train bound for Michigan and other points east.

A moment that will shape our family destiny for generations occurs a couple days later in the Desnoyer Funeral Home in Jackson. The dead priest's brother, my grandfather, is meeting with the undertaker to sort details for the hometown funeral at St. John's. He brings along my father, now gone twelve, for reasons we can never know. While the two men are discussing plots and boxes, pallbearers and honoraria, the boy wanders through the old mortuary until he comes to the doorway of a room where he espies two men in shirtsleeves dressing a corpse in liturgical vestments. He stands and watches quietly. Then they carefully lift the freshly vested body of his dead uncle from the white porcelain table into a coffin. Then turn to see the boy at the door. Ever after my father will describe this moment—this elevation, this slow, almost ritual hefting of the body—as the one to which he will always trace his intention to become a funeral director. Might it have aligned in his imagination with that moment during the Masses he attended at St. Francis De Sales when the priest would elevate the host and chalice, the putative body and blood of Christ, when bells were rung, heads bowed, breasts beaten in awe? Might he have conflated the corruptible and the incorruptible? The mortal and immortality? The sacred and the profane?

"Why," we would often ask him, "why didn't you decide to become a priest?"

"Well," he would tell us, matter-of-factly, "the priest was dead."

It was also true that he'd met Rosemary O'Hara that year, a redheaded fifth-grader who would become the girl of his dreams and who would write him daily when he went off to war with the Marines in the South Pacific, who would marry him when he came home and mother their nine children, and beside whom he'd be buried half a century later.

"God works in strange ways," my mother would tell us, smiling wisely, passing the spuds, all of us marveling at the ways of things.

And so these "callings," such as they were, these summons to her life as a wife and mother and his to fatherhood and undertaking—a life's work he would always describe as "serving the living by caring for the dead" or a "corporal work of mercy"—and his sons' and daughters' and their sons and daughters who operate now half a dozen funeral homes in towns all over lower Michigan, all tied to that first week of August 1936 and a boy watching two mortuary sorts lift the body of a dead priest into a box.

That was another received truth of his nunnish upbringing and our own—that life and time were not random accretions of happenstance. On the contrary, there was a plan for each and every one of us and ours was only to discern our "vocation," our "calling," our purpose here. No doubt this is how the life of faith, the search for meaning, the wonder about the way of things first sidles up to the curious mind.

———

When I was seven, my mother sent me off to see the priest, to learn enough of the magic Latin—the language of ritual and mystery—to become an altar boy. Fr. Kenny, our parish priest at St. Columban's, was a native of Galway and had been at seminary with my father's uncle and hatched a plan with my sainted mother to guide me toward the holy orders. This, the two of them no doubt reckoned, was in keeping with the Will of God—that I should fulfill the vocation and finish the work of the croupy and tubercular young man I'd been named for. I looked passably hallowed in cassock and surplice, I had a knack for the vowel-rich acoustics of Latin and had already intuited the accountancy of sin and guilt and shame and punishment so central to the religious life. This tuition I owed to *Father Maguire's Baltimore Catechism* and the Sister Servants of the Immaculate Heart of Mary who had prepared me for the grade school sacraments of Confession and the Eucharist. I had learned to fast before communion, to confess and do penance in preparation for the feast, to keep track of my sins by sort and number, to purge them by prayer and mortification, supplication and petition. To repair the damage done by impure thoughts or cursing at a sibling, a penance of Our Fathers and Hail Marys would be assigned. *Mea culpa, mea culpa, mea maxima culpa* became for me the breast thumping idioms of forgiveness and food, purification and communion, atonement and satiety, reconciliation and recompense which are so central to the "holy sacrifice of

the Mass" we Catholic school kids daily attended. Thus were
the connections between hunger and holiness, blight and
blessedness, contrition and redemption, early on established,
and these powerful religious metaphors gathered themselves
around the common table. That sacred theater replayed itself
each night at our family meals where our father and our
blessed mother would enact a home version of the sacrifice
and feast, the brothers and sisters and I returning prodigals
for whom the fatted calf, incarnate as stew or goulash, burgers
or casseroles, had been prepared. On Fridays my father
brought home bags of fish and chips. Whatever our sins were,
they seemed forgiven.

Introibo ad altare Dei is what James Joyce had "stately, plump
Buck Mulligan" intone on the opening page of his epic
Ulysses, holding a bowl of lather aloft, and years later, reading
that book for the first time, *Ad deum qui laetificat juventutem
meam* still formed in my memory as the cadenced response to
the gods who'd given joy to my youth. Irreverence seemed a
proper seasoning by then, the grain of salt added to articles of
faith. I'd come to love the sound of religion—its plain chants
and Gregorians, the rhymed and metered and repeated
prayers, the magic of Latin spoken and sung, the code words
and arcana. But I'd begun to question the sense of it all—the
legalisms and accountancy by which glorious and sorrowful
mysteries were rendered a sort of dogmatic and dispassionate
math. To be so certain about God struck me as sacrilege. Faith
must be more than religious belief and obedience.

Argyle comes by his irreverence honestly. The animus borne
toward Argyle by the families of the dead—the "whispering
contempts" amid which he performs his hungry offices—is
replicated by the reverend clergy who regard him as an upstart
and forger, a pretender to the throne of their authority. As

purveyors of moral order and suasion, religious practice and forgiveness, churchmen quite rightly see sin-eating as unholy competition. What need has the sinner of the sacraments when forgiveness can be so cheaply purchased? What need of tithing when sin-eating can be got for a "pay as you go" stipendium of bread and beer and sixpence? Because both commoners and clergy hold him in low esteem, Argyle is banished to the hinterlands of the social and moral order. The wound of this estrangement, which works its way through the narrative of these poems in the resentments Argyle voices toward the authority of the church, is akin to the contentions that inform the history of schism, reformation, division, and denomination about which St. Paul wrote to no avail to the Corinthians in the first century and John XXIII and my late grandmother addressed in the last. We are all—every being in creation— hungry for the favor of our creator. We all believe that God is on our side. And yet all of us know the pain of not belonging, the cruel isolation of the shunned and excommunicant. Still, if begrudgery is contagious, so is gratitude. And Argyle concludes that to be forgiven we must forgive, everyone and everything. Grace is undeserved and abundant and, despite his foibles and those of his fellow sinners among both clergy and commoners, Argyle comes to see them all as fellow pilgrims, at times ridiculous, at times sublime, but always beloved of God.

For all of my mother's and the priest's well-intentioned connivances, and though I kept my ears peeled for it, I never ever heard the voice of God. I remember seeing the dead priest's cassock hanging from a rafter in my grandparents' basement, a box with his biretta and other priestly things on a shelf beside it. I tried them on but nothing seemed to fit and over time my life of faith came to include an ambivalence about the church which ranged from passion to indifference—a kind of swithering, brought on, no doubt, by mighty nature—the certain sense awakened in me when I was twelve or thereabouts that among the good lord's greatest gifts to humankind were the gifts he gave us of each other. Possibly it was meditating on the changes I could see in bodies all around me and sense in my own body, late in my grade-school years, that there were aspects of the priestly life that would be, thanks be to God, impossible for me.

I record these things because they seem somehow the ground and compost out of which Argyle rose, in that flash of recognition years ago, to become the mouthpiece for my mixed religious feelings. If I'd learned sin and guilt and shame and contrition from the nuns and priests, I was likewise schooled in approval and tolerance and inextinguishable love by my parents, earthen vessels though they were. Grace—the unmerited favor of Whoever Is In Charge Here—was the gift outright of my upbringing. It made me, like the apostle the priest I'd been named for was named for, a doubter and contrarian— grateful for religious sensibilities but wary of all magisteriums.

By the end of winter that first year I'd written three or four Argyle poems. I field-tested them at Joe's Star Lounge on North Main Street in Ann Arbor, where boozers and poets would gather on Sunday afternoons to read their latest to one another. It was a kind of communion, I suppose, or potluck anyway: everyone bringing a "dish" to pass, their best home recipes of words. I liked the sound of them in my mouth, the cadence of Argyle's odd adventures and little blasphemies.

His name came easy, after the socks, of course, the only thing I knew that was reliably Scots, apart from whiskey, and the acoustic resemblance to "our guile," which sounded a note not far from "guilt," both notions that attached them- selves to his invention.

These were the days long before one could Google up facts
on demand, when writers were expected to just make things
up out of the whole cloth of imagination: his loneliness,
the contempt of locals, the contretemps of clergy—I
intuited these, along with the sense of his rootlessness, his
orphanage and pilgrimage. I'd spent, by then, enough time
in the rural western parishes of Ireland and Scotland to
have a sense of the landscapes and people he would find
himself among—their "ground sense" and land passions,
their religious sensibilities. And the two dozen lines of the
first of these poems, each of the lines ranging between nine
and a dozen syllables and thus conforming to a imprecise
pentameter, seemed perfectly suited to the brief meditations
and reliance on numbers and counts that were part of the
churchy rubrics: stations of the cross, deadly sins, glorious
and sorrowful mysteries, corporal and spiritual works of
mercy, the book of hours. Hence this breviary: a couple
dozen poems, a couple dozen lines each, a couple dozen
photos.

By turns, of course, I began to identify with Argyle. As
the only funeral director in a small town in Michigan, I was
aware of the ambivalence of human sorts toward anyone who
takes on undertakings involving money and corpses, religious
practice and residual guilt. Both undertaker and sin-eater
know that people in need are glad to see you coming and
gladder still to see you gone. No less is true of the curate and
parish priest with whom Argyle identifies, yet finds himself
at odds. I was likewise aware of the occasional awkwardness
between mortuary sorts and the reverend clergy. No few of
the latter would quite rightly wince at the crass mercantilism
of no few of the former who would, in turn, roll their eyes at
the human failings of the latter.

"That's just not necessary," a churchman once complained to my father in reference to a pricey casket that had been chosen by a congregant's family and rolled into church.

"Neither is any of that," replied my dad, nodding at the stained glass and mosaics, vaulted ceilings and statuary.

And yet, over time, both pastor and dismal trader come to appreciate the humanity of the other, the willingness to show up in the worst of circumstances, outfitted with only a willingness to serve.

Argyle fit my purposes and circumstances. The work to which he had, by force of hunger, been called, seemed in concert with my own summons and stumblings both religiously and occupationally. He is trying to keep body and soul together. And he articulates the mixed blessing and contrariety of my own life of faith—pre–Vatican II to the Current Sadness—through which I have been variously devout and devoutly lapsed.

Among the blessings of forty years of work as a funeral director is that it has put me in earshot of the reverend clergy trying to make sense of senseless things: the man who kills his wife, their poodle, then himself; a mother who drowns her baby then does her nails; the teenager with the broken heart and loaded pistol; the tumors and emboli, flues and tsunamis, deadly contagions and misadventures—the endless renditions of The Book of Job. When someone shows up—priest or pastor, rabbi or imam, venerable master or fellow traveler—to stand with the living and the dead and speak into the gaping maw of the unspeakable, I know I am witnessing uncommon courage and my perennially shaken faith is emboldened by theirs.

"Behold, I show you a mystery," they always say. They are balm and anointing, these men and women of God, frontline infantry and holy corpsmen in the wars long waged between faith and fear.

And yet, among the lessons of four decades of travel between Holy Ireland and my home in Michigan is that the church has long suffered from mostly self-inflicted wounds, and mostly at the hands of upper echelon sorts.

Of course, the life of faith is never settled, driven as it must be by doubts and wonder, by those experiences, losses and griefs, that cast us adrift, set us to wander the deserts, wrestle with angels. And for Argyle, as for all fellow pilgrims, the tensions between community and marginalization, orthodoxy and apostasy, authority and autonomy, belonging and disbelief, keep him forever second-guessing where he stands with God. In this state of flux he is not alone.

The sin-eater is both appalled by his culture's religiosity and beholden to it. The accountancy of sin and punishment at once offends him and feeds him. He is caught in the struggle between views of damnation and salvation and the God he imagines as the loving parents he never knew—pure forgiveness, constant understanding, permanent love. He lives in constant hope and fear, despair and faith, gratitude and God hunger. In the end he isn't certain but believes that everything is forgiven, whomever God is or isn't, everything is reconciled.

If the English master, Auden, was correct, and "art is what we do to break bread with the dead," then the Irish master, Heaney, was likewise correct when he suggests that "rhyme and meter are the table manners." Prayer and poetry are both forms of "raised speech" by which we attempt to commune with our makers and creation, with the gone but not forgotten. Argyle's hunger, his breaking bread upon the dead, is a metaphor for all those rituals and rubrics by which our kind seeks to commune with those by whom we are haunted—the ghosts of those gone before us, parents and lovers, mentors and heroes, friends and fellow outcasts, who share with us this sweet humanity, our little moments, the sense we are always trying to make of it in words. His is a sacrament of renewal and restoration. It is in such communion that our hope is nourished—the hope that is signature to our species—that there may be something in nature's harmonium and hush discernible as the voice of God.

Much the same with icon and image—the things we see in which we might see other things, the hand of God or the hand of man partaking in the same creation. Thus these photographs, taken by my son Michael in his many visits to our home in Ireland—the house his great-great-grandfather came out of, the house to which I was the first of our family to return, now more than forty years ago, the house my great-great-grandfather was given as a wedding gift in the decade after the worst of the famines in the middle of the nineteenth century.

When I first went to Ireland—a young man with a high number in the Nixon draft lotto and, therefore, a future stretched out before me—I thought I'd see the forty shades of green. And though I arrived in the off-season, with a one-way ticket, no money or prospects, in a poor county of a poor country, as disappointing a yank as ever there was, I was welcomed by cousins who could connect me to the photo that hung on their wall of their cousin, a priest, who had died years before. They took me in, put me by the fire, fed me, and gave me to believe that I belonged there, I was home. If there is a heaven it might feel like that. In the fullness of time, they left the house to me: a gift, a grace. Everything in those times seemed so black and white—the cattle, the clergy, the stars and dark, right and wrong, love and hate,

the edges and borders all well defined. But now it all seems
like shades of grey, shadow and apparition, glimpses only,
through the half-light of daybreak and gloaming, mirage
and apocalypse, a kind of *swithering*. And so these photos of
home fires and icons, landscapes and interiors, graveyards
and coast roads, asses and cattle, statues and stone haunts—
all in black and white and shades of grey: like doubt and
faith, what may or mayn't be, what is or isn't, happenstance
or the hand of God.

———

In the end, Argyle is just trying to find his way home.
Burdened by mighty nature, life's work and tuitions, he's
looking for a place at a table where he is always welcome
and never alone. Possessed of few certainties or absolutes, his
faith always seasoned by wonder and doubt, he knows if there's
a god, it is not him. He knows if there is one, then surely we
are all God's children, or none of us are. He knows the greatest
gifts are one another, the greatest sins against each other. To
be forgiven, he must forgive everything, because God forgives
everything or nothing at all, hears all our prayers or none of
them.

At the end, all of his prayers begin to sound like *thanks*. All of
the answers have become *you're welcome*.

TL
November 2, 2010

THE
Sin-eater

A BREVIARY

FRIESANS MOVEEN

The Sin-eater

Argyle the sin-eater came the day after—
a narrow, hungry man whose laughter
and the wicked upturn of his one eyebrow
put the local folks in mind of trouble.
But still they sent for him and sat him down
amid their whispering contempts to make
his table near the dead man's middle,
and brought him soda bread and bowls of beer
and candles, which he lit against the reek
that rose off that impenitent cadaver
though bound in skins and soaked in rosewater.
Argyle eased the warm loaf right and left
and downed swift gulps of beer and venial sin
then lit into the bread now leavened with
the corpse's cardinal mischiefs, then he said
"Six pence, I'm sorry." And the widow paid him.
Argyle took his leave then, down the land
between hay-ricks and Friesians with their calves
considering the innocence in all
God's manifold creation but for Man,
and how he'd perish but for sin and mourning.
Two parishes between here and the ocean:
a bellyful tonight is what he thought,
please God, and breakfast in the morning.

CHURCH INTERIOR WEST CLARE

Argyle in Agony

Some sins Argyle couldn't stomach much.
Sins against virgin girls and animals,
women bearing children, men gone blind
from all but self-abusive reasons gave him
stomach troubles, like over seasoned meat
he oughtn't to have eaten, but he always did.
Some nights those evils woke him in his sleep,
gaseous and flatulent, bent over his puke bowl,
resolved again to draw the line somewhere,
to leave the dirty work to younger men,
or anyway, to up his prices.
Maybe steady work with nuns whose vices
were rumored to go down like tapioca.
But no, those clever ladies lived forever
and for all their charities would starve the man
who counted for his feed on their transgressions.
Better to go on as he always had,
eating sins and giving souls their blessed rest.
What matter that his innards heaved against
a steady diet of iniquities
or that children worked their mayhem on his head
by carving pumpkins up in fearful effigies?
He had his holy orders and his mission.
He had the extreme unction of his daily bread.

TURF SHED MOVEEN

Argyle's Vapors

Vaporous and sore at heart, Argyle
stood in his doorway looking out at nothing.
The wind blew through him as if he wasn't.
As if he were, himself, a door ajar
through which one had to go to get nowhere
and wanting to go nowhere, there he stood—
a spectacle of shortfall and desire.
And all the voice of reason in him reasoned was
"Take heart, Argyle! This is seasonal.
The winter is a cruel but equal cross
borne only by the living in the name of Christ,
and though a cold encumbrance on the soul afire
with ministry and purpose, bear in mind
the dead will keep for days in such weather
and any climate so kind to a corpse
will shorten purgatory for those left alive
to huddle in their mud and wattles for some warmth."
Such comfort as that gave him helped him weather
well enough the chill and shortened days,
the noise of rats wintering in his thatch,
the endless bitter merriment at wakes.
By dark he dreamed the touch of female flesh—
all night in sweats and brimming scenes of pleasure—
and waking up alone, he blamed the weather.

TOWER HOUSE

Argyle's Balance

Argyle kept his balance feeling himself
between two equal and opposing forces,
each, at once, both fearsome and endearing.
He had dreams. In one a woman in her bright flesh
kneels in the river, bathing. Later, she
lies in the tall grass drying, reddening
her nipples with the juice of pomegranates,
offering them and her body to him.
This was his dream of youth and lovemaking,
of greensong, water, all life-giving things.
The other was a dream of himself, in
extremis. The children gather, dumbstruck
at his belly, bulbous with flatus, fat
with the old sins of others and his own.
A priest stands ready with chrisms and forgiveness.
He always dreamt this after radishes.
These were the horizontal mysteries
from either one of which he would arise
breathless with intimacy and release,
invigored with deliverance, alive.
The answer he figured was to keep an arm's reach
between his waking self and either dream, listing
only slightly from upright anytime
the dreams made music and he would listen.

9

BRONZE GIRL KILBAHA

Argyle's Ejaculations

Argyle's preference in sins was legend.
The best of them were those the priests invented:
broken fasts or abstinence in Lent,
a tithe unpaid or Sunday morning passed
in honest, gainful labor or in bed.
He feasted full on Easter Duties missed
or some bad-mouthing of a Jesuit.
He relished churchy sins that had no flesh
or blood or bones, but only upset
some curate's dictum on moral etiquette.
"God Bless His Holiness in Rome, O Lord!"—
Argyle often ejaculated—
"And all Right Reverend Eminence & Graces,
and all the idle time they have to kill
concocting new sins for my evening meal."
But then he'd dream that girl-child again,
defiled by some mannish violence who threw
herself to death, despairing, down a bog hole.
And when the parish house refused her requiems,
her people sent for Argyle to come
and undo by his dinner what the girl had done.
But Argyle knelt and wept and refused the bread,
and poured the bowl of bitters on the ground
and prayed, "God spare my hunger till that churchman's dead."

CUCHULAIN'S LEAP LOOP HEAD

Argyle's Retreat

Great hosts of basking sharks and shoals of mackerel,
like breathren in the one Creation, swam
together in the seas around Loop Head Point,
free of those long-standing habits of predation
whereby the larger fellow eats the small.
In Kilkee church, two girls saw statues move.
Lights appeared and disappeared and reappeared
from Doonaghboy to Newtown and the dead were seen
perched upon ditchbanks with their turnip lamps by night.
In Moveen, cattle sang, crows barked, and kittens flew.
The tidal pools at Goleen filled with blood
and all the common wisdoms were undone
by signs and wonders everywhere. Argyle
wondered were they miracles or omens?
God's handiwork or some bedevilment
called up or down on him by that avenging priest
he'd lately tangled with? Either way, retreat
was the word that formed in him. A fortnight's rest
at Dingle, fast and prayer to purge and cleanse himself
among those holy hermits there who never
once, for all their vast privations, ever
saw or heard a thing or apprehended God
abounding in their stars or stones or seas.
And for all they hadn't witnessed, yet believed.

THE SEA AT ROSS

Argyle's Dream of the Churchdove

Argyle saw the Inner Hebrides
in dreams and dozings, spasms of the light
in which the vision under eyelids brightened
the dark precincts of ancient memory.
Iona in his father's father's time . . .
His father's father singing to the sea
a lamentation of his own mad making
aside the strand where blessed Columcille
first landed with his boats and brother monks
and looking back fro Ulster couldn't see
beyond the thickening pale of exile.
O ancient gray-eyed saint—the old one sang—
old sire of my bastard lineage,
please intercede with God to send a Sign
that I might know my bilious ministry
serves both the sinner and The Sinned Against!
At that a churchdove flew out of the fog
and striving skyward, shat upon his head,
the bird's anointing oozing into each
and every sensing orifice he had.
And shaken by the vision, Argyle,
uncertain of its meaning, nonetheless,
woke mouthing words of praise and wonderment
in fiery tongues, remarkable and strange.

IRONMONGER'S TRIPTYCH

Argyle in Carrigaholt

At Carrigaholt the priest was famous for
the loud abhorrence that he preached against
adherence to the ancient superstitions.
Old cures, evil eyes and hocus-pocuses
were banned as unholy forms of competition.
"The divil," he'd say, then something Latin
the townspeople took to mean anathema,
whenever the tinkers turned up in their wagons
full of charms and spells and red-haired daughters
telling fortunes and selling talismans.
Argyle got there quite by accident—
a wrong turn on the coastal road en route
to Loop Head where a sinner lay stone-dead
by dint of the eighty-some-odd years he'd lived
on that peninsula. But when the priest got wind
of it, he sent his acolytes to bring
the sin-eater in for inquisitioning.
And Argyle humored him all night until
the priest made threats of holy violence,
to which Argyle, grinning, said, "Good priest, relent.
You do a brisk trade in indulgences
and tithes and votive lamps and requiems.
You keep your pope and robes and host and chalice.
Leave me my loaf and bowl and taste for malice."

ILLANANARUEN

Argyle's Return to the Holy Island

After the dream of the churchdove and the tongues,
Argyle contemplated pilgrimage
to that blessed island in the Hebrides
from which his ancient lineage had sprung
from the sainted loinage of Columbans
whose couplings with the island women left
a legacy of zealotry, God-hunger,
genius and the occasional idiot
that worked its way down blighted centuries
of monks and anchorites and sin-eaters—
a race of men much gifted with their mouths
for giving out with prayers and poetry
or, like Argyle, for the eating of
sinful excess, shortfalls, mediocrities,
such as would set most lesser men to vomiting.
With neither mule nor map, Argyle walked
aimlessly throughout the western places
until he came to water which he crossed
from island to smaller island praising
the fierce weather, the full moon, the faithful boatmen.
What makes this aching in the soul? he thought,
for distant islands where the silence hordes
the voices of our dead among the stones?
And though no answer was forthcoming he went forth.

GLOR NA MARA

Argyle's Stone

Around his neck Argyle wore a stone:
green marble from the strand at Iona
where Columcille and his banished kinsmen
landed after bloody Cooldrevny claimed
three thousand in 561 AD.
"To every cow its calf; to books their copy!"—
the notion that begat that savagery.
His ruminations on such histories
put him in mind of how most mortals kept
committing the same sin over and over
like calving cows or Psalter manuscripts—
each a version of the original.
Among his pendant stone's known properties:
general healing, protection from fire,
shipwreck, miscarriage and other dire
possibilities that might imperil
a pilgrim of Argyle's appetites.
Foremost among the sin-eater's lapses
were hunger, which was constant, and then thirst,
and all known iterations of desire—
craving and coveting, lusting and glut:
whatever was was never quite enough.
So for ballast among such gravities
Argyle wore the stone; for anchorage.

KILBALLYOWEN

Argyle at Loop Head

Argyle kept to the outposts and edges,
cliff rocks, coastal roads, estuary banks,
sheltering in dry ditches, thick hedges,
forts and cabin ruins, beside stone ranks,
much scorned by men, much put-upon by weather.
The weeping of keeners brought him hither,
fresh grief, fresh graves, lights in dark localities—
such signs and wonders of mortality
drew him towards the living and the dead
to foment pardon in a bowl of beer
or leaven remission out of common bread,
and when his feast was finished, disappear.
The bodies of the dead he dined over
never troubled Argyle but still
their souls went with him into exile
and, reincarnate as gulls and plovers,
dove from high headlands over the ocean
in fits of hopeful flight, much as heaven
was said to require a leap of faith
into the fathomless and unbeknownst.
Sometimes the urge to follow them was so
near overwhelming he could almost taste
the loss of gravity in brackish air,
his leap, the sea's embrace, his savior.

STONE INTERIOR KILBAHA

Argyle's Eucharist

Upright over corpses it occurred to him—
the body outstretched on a pair of planks,
the measly loaf and stingy goblet,
the gobsmacked locals, their begrudging thanks,
the kinswomen rummaging for coppers—
it came into his brain like candlelight:
his lot in life like priesthood after all.
Such consolations as the kind he proffered,
by sup and gulp consuming mortals' sins,
quenching hellfire, dousing purgatory,
transforming requiems to baptismals;
but for holy orders and a church,
bells and vestments and lectionary,
a bishop, benefice or sinecure,
the miracles were more or less the same:
a transubstantiation, sleight and feint,
a reconfiguration of accounts
whereby he took unto himself the woe
that ought betide the rotting decadent.
Perdition due the recent decedent
thus averted by Argyle's hunger,
the unencumbered soul makes safe to God,
the decomposing dead get buried under
earth and stone. The sin-eater belches, wipes his gob.

HAGGARD WALL MOVEEN

A Corporal Work of Mercy

"God bless all here, the living and the dead!"
Thus spake Argyle ducking through the door.
A woman's corpse outstretched on the stone floor
was yellow jaundiced and so corpulent
the wizened man hunched sobbing next to it
in deep paroxysms of grief and shame
could neither hoist her on the table nor
drag the fat cadaver from the place.
So setting candles at her head and feet
he'd kept the vigil raising his lament
whilst praying for sufficient aid to move her
before he was evicted by the stench.
Argyle, moved by such entreaties bent
such powers as he had to the removal,
taking up those huge shanks by the ankles
he hauled away and the husband pushed her.
After half a morning's massive labors
they'd got her out the back door to the haggard—
a heap among the spuds and cabbages
of putrefaction and composting grief—
and knowing that the job was incomplete
they set to work with spades and dug a ditch
of such surpassing depth and length and breadth . . .
it was after dark they shoved her into it.

SUPPLICANTS MOVEEN

Argyle Considers the Elements

Argyle surveyed the ominous maw
of tempest assembling off Kilbaha
in the pike's Mouth of the River Shannon,
obscuring the white strand at Ballybunion
and County Kerry's western expanses:
the lay of the land in all directions
blackened with calamity's sure advance.
The sin eater, given to introspection,
wondered was it something he ate or drank
over the grey corpse of a publican
the night before in Kilballyowen.
Possibly, a sinfulness so grotesque
even his scapegoating could not redress it
and so the heavens would themselves exact
prompt compensation through an Act of God:
whirlwind, maelstrom, lightning and thunderclap,
fissure or freak wave, black frost or flashflood—
he'd seen this balancing of books before.
The bishop of Galway was swallowed whole,
swept off the planet by a cataract
and gobbled up by the sea's upheaval—
something to do with a woman and her boy
against whose innocence he had inveighed.
No glimpse of him was ever got again.

MOYARTA

Argyle Among the Moveen Lads

The Moveen lads were opening a grave
in Moyarta, for Porrig O'Loinsigh,
got dead in his cow cabin in between two
Friesans, their udders bursting, his face gone blue.
"As good a way to go as any, faith,"
said Canon McMahon the parish priest.
"Sure, wasn't our savior born in such a place?"
Unmoved by which rhetorical, the lads
kept mum but for their picks and spades which rang
out their keen begrudgeries and gratitudes.
"God spare the labor and the laborers!"
So quoth Argyle, passing in the road.
"The last among the earthen decencies—
this shovel and shoulder work by which are borne
our fellow pilgrims on their journeys home."
Uplifted by which utterance, the lads
proffered whiskey, gobeens of local cheese,
a cut of plug tobacco. "Take your ease
with us awhile," said one, "here among the bones
of the dead man's elders buried years ago,
now resurrected by our excavations."
And there among old stones his contemplations
hovered among femurs and holding up a skull,
"Alas," he said, "O'Loinsigh, I knew him well!"

HOMEFIRE

His Ambulations

On shanks' mare Argyle talked to himself.
Alone, he'd carry on whole colloquies
en route to some poor corpse's obsequies—
these dialogues, the way he kept his wits
about him, body and soul together,
fit for the wretched work of sin-eating.
Sometimes he counted words or parts of words
as if they amounted to something more
than sound and sense attuned between his ears,
as, for example, how coincident:
the way *grace* and *gratis*, wherefore *gratitude*
partook a kinship such as cousins do,
singing the same tune in different voices,
much as *grave* and *gravitas*, then *gravity*
kept one earthbound, grounded, humble as the mud—
the *humus*, so-called, God wrought *humans* from.
Or how from Adam's rib was fashioned Eve—
bone of his own bone, flesh of his flesh—
whom he got *gravid* by implanting seed,
in her unfathomably fecund Eden.
The memory of a woman's company
would bring his ambulations to a halt
to aim his gaping face due heavenward,
the dewy air her touch, her taste, sweet salt.

33

PIEBALDS AT FEED

His Repasts

He ate the boiled breakfast and the fry—
rashers and puddings, eggs and porridge oats,
late tea with milk and sugar, every night
he could get it, some nights a lump of goat's
cheese or sausage with it. Such were his habits.
As for the dinner, long accreted sins
served up with corpses and a gainful wage
(in keeping with his station and remit)
were all that ever really satisfied.
Tough work, alas, still someone had to do it.
No less the mutes and watchers, wailing hags,
who kept their vigils at all local wakes
beating their breasts, enacting pantomimes,
waiting to see in case the dead would rise
to the occasion: spirits and soul cakes.
Whereupon the reverend curate's narrative
of how the poor cratur was yet alive
and writhing no doubt in purgatory
would haunt the living through the dark of night.
Mid-morning's when Argyle would arrive
and for a fraction of the churchman's fee,
he'd tender sweet remission, clean the plate
of every crumb and drain the tankard.
The dead, thus left to their contingencies,
the living carried on their theatres.

THOOR BALLYLEE

He Considers Not the Lilies
but Their Excellencies

Thin gruel, shallow graves, whiskey watered down,
the ne'er-do-well and good-for-nothing crowd
of cornerboys and gobshites were among
Argyle's manifold perturbations.
Worse still, the episcopal vexations:
their excellencies, eminence and graces,
red cassocked dandies and mitered wankers,
the croziered posers in their bishoprics
with their Easter duties and Peters pence,
their ledgers full of mortal, venial sins—
keepers of the till and tally, bankers
of indulgences and dispensations;
their bulls and bans and excommunications,
nothing but contumely and bamboozles.
For all their vestiture, rings and unctions,
preaching to bishops, like farting at skunks, was
nothing but a mug's game to the sin-eater,
so in earshot of them mum is what he kept.
Still, he thought there might be something to it:
a life apart from this life where the souls
long dead and gone were neither dead nor gone.
Some days he felt so happily haunted,
by loving ghosts and gods upholding him.
Some days he felt entirely alone.

O'DONOHUE'S HEART, FANORE, THE BURREN

He Weeps Among the Clare Antiquities

At Poulnabrone Dolmen Argyle poured
his soul's ache into the hole of sorrows,
huddling under the ancient capstone
against the cold and crueler elements.
Stone portal, stone cairn, stone everywhere—
the rocky desert of the Burren bore
a semblance to his own hard-weathered heart
made barren by years of cast aspersions, pox,
maledictions, cursed lonliness and loss.
Only by wretching over the earth's bone box,
or pissing on the effigy at Corcomroe
or making for the graveyard at Fanore
to visit his late, great confessor's tomb—
(the druid holy man, O'Donohue's)—
could he purge himself of bile and rancor
so, this twice or thrice a yearly pilgrimage
up the West Clare coast and down again
lightened the load of comeuppance his grim
work among the newly dead occasioned.
Among old stones a calm came over him
as if the dead beneath them held their own
redemptions on their journeys heavenward,
like wild flowers gathered out of bones,
their sweet bouquets a comfort beyond words.

WINDING STAIRS

Argyle at the Ennis Friary

Among the friars minor Argyle
kept his silence and meditations on
the joyous and sorrowful mysteries,
and dwelt on Transitus—the holy soul's
last pilgrimage—in imitation of
the saint's embrace of Sister Death, in Assisi
the third of October, 1226.
Argyle prayed to purge his dreams of sex
with minoresses in their brown habits,
busy at their blessedness, their sweet breasts
swelling under scapulars, their fine hands
always at the work of heaven, their hush
a constant prayer for continence of flesh,
as Poor Clare's order had accustomed them
to poverty, chastity, obedience.
Godhelp Argyle, he could not help himself:
for all his pieties and flagellations,
the taste of Sister Mary on his tongue,
the touch of her fingers on his person
the safe hold and harbor of her body
became the icons of his supplications;
to lie as Francis had, naked and alone,
just once before the end, and to show her
the love of God such as he'd come to know it.

CLIFFS AND STANDING STONE

He Posits Certain Mysteries

The body of the boy who took his flight
off the cliff at Kilcloher into the sea
was hauled up by curragh-men, out at first light
fishing mackerel in the estuary.
"No requiem or rosary" said the priest,
"nor consecrated ground for burial,"
as if the boy had flown outside the pale
of mercy or redemption or God's love.
"Forgive them, for they know not what they do,"
quoth Argyle to the corpse's people,
who heard in what he said a sort of riddle,
as if he meant their coreligionists
and not their sodden, sadly broken boy.
Either way, they took some comfort in it
and readied better than accustomed fare
of food and spirits; by their own reckoning:
the greater sin, the greater so the toll.
But Argyle refused their shilling coin
and helped them build a box and dig a grave.
"Your boy's no profligate or prodigal,"
he said, "only a wounded pilgrim like us all.
What say his leaping was a leap of faith,
into his father's beckoning embrace?"
They killed no fatted calf. They filled the hole.

43

MADONNA MOVEEN

His Purgations

Argyle shat himself and, truth be told,
but for the mess of it, the purging was
no bad thing for the body corporal.
Would that the soul were so thoroughly cleansed,
by squatting and grunting supplications.
Would that purgatories and damnations
could be so quickly doused and recompensed,
null and voided in the name of mercy.
He made for Goleen and a proper laving
of his crotch and loins and paltry raiments.
Outstretched on the strand, his body's immersion
in the tide was not unlike a christening:
two goats for godparents, two herring gulls
perched in the current his blessed parents,
a fat black cormorant the parish priest
anointing him with chrisms and oils,
pronouncing him reborn, renamed, renewed
in the living waters of baptism.
In every dream he dreamt after bathing,
the guilt and guile of his sin eating
and all accrued perditions were absolved
and he was named after an apostle
or martyr or evangelist or saint,
welcome everywhere, forgiven everything.

PENINSULA

Argyle on Knocknagaroon

Because he barely heard the voice of God
above the tune of other choristers—
batwing and bird-whistle, gathering thunder,
the hiss of tides retreating, children, cattle;
because he could not readily discern
the plan Whoever Is In Charge Here has,
he wondered about those who claimed to have
blessed assurances or certainty:
a One and Only Way and Truth and Life,
as if Whatever Breathes in Everything
mightn't speak in every wondrous tongue;
as if, of all creations, only one
made any sense. It made no sense to him.
Hunger he understood, touch, desire.
He knew the tenderness humans could do,
no less brutalities. He knew the cold
morning, the broad meadow, the gold sunset.
One evening on the hill of Knocknagaroon,
the Atlantic on one side, the Shannon
on the other, the narrowing headlands
of the peninsula out behind him,
the broad green palm of Moveen before him,
it seemed he occupied the hand of God:
open, upturned, outstretched, uplifting him.

PARACLETE MOVEEN

Recompense His Paraclete

His paraclete was a piebald donkey
bequeathed him by a sad-eyed parish priest
whose sins he supped away one Whitsunday
some months in advance of your man's demise.
"Never a shortage of asses, Argyle,
God knows we've all got one of them at least."
Which truth seemed surplus to requirements.
Argyle named the wee jack Recompense
and got good orderly direction from it.
Wherever the one went, so went the other
bearing mighty nature's burdens wordlessly,
the brown sign of the cross across their backs.
The last was ever seen of them was headed west—
a tatterdemalion and his factotum—
making for the coast road in the cold and gloaming,
braying and flailing out gestures of blessing
over hedgerow and hay-bales, man and beast
alike, hovel and out-office, dung-heap and home,
everything in eye and earshot rectified:
cats pardoned, curs absolved, tethered cattle loosed,
and all of vast creation reconciled
in one last spasm of forgiveness.
As for the sin-eater and Recompense,
where the road turned toward the sea they turned with it.

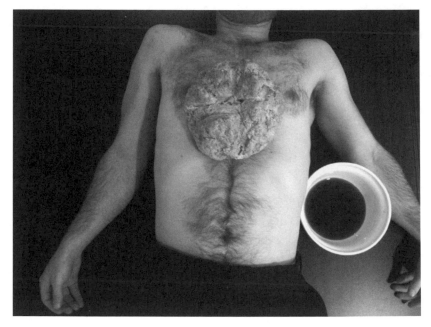

LOAF AND BOWL

Notes on Photos

The photographs that accompany these poems, all taken by Michael Lynch with cameras ranging from a Canon 10D to an IPhone HD, like the landscapes and place names that inform the poems, are all situate in the West of Ireland, on the West Clare Peninsula that narrows between the North Atlantic and the Shannon Estuary.

Several of these photos, including "Kitchen Shrine Moveen," "Friesans Moveen," "Turf Shed Moveen," "Haggard Wall Moveen," "Supplicants Moveen," and "Homefire," were taken in or around the author's ancestral home in the townland of Moveen, near Kilkee, County Clare. This is the home-place that Thomas Curry Lynch left in 1890 when he emigrated through Canada to Jackson, Michigan. His great-grandson, Thomas Lynch, was the first of his line to return to Ireland, in February of 1970. The author inherited the house from his second cousin, Nora Lynch, at her death in 1992. He and his family spend portions of each year in residence there. Other photos include:

"Church Interior West Clare" Our Lady, Star of the Sea, Church at Quilty, County Clare.

"Tower House" O'Brien's Tower (1835) at Moher, County Clare

"Bronze Girl Kilbaha" Public sculpture based on Diarmid and Grainne by Jim Connolly, Kilbaha, County Clare.

"Cuchulain's Leap Loop Head" Standing stone rookery off Loop Head that figures in the heroic stories of lovers in pursuit, who leapt the space between mainland and island, some with more success than others.

"The Sea at Ross" Natural stone bridges and sea ledges at Ross, near Loop Head, County Clare.

"Ironmonger's Triptych" Public iron and glass sculpture at Kilbaha, County Clare, wrought by Paddy Murray, teacher and artist, Kilkee, County Clare; panels: (top) The Ark at Kilbaha, (middle) Kitchen Scene, and (bottom) Church Ruins at Kilballyowen.

"Illananaruen" Also known as Murray's Island, off the Atlantic coast of West Clare.

"Glor na Mara" Voice of the Sea, stone boat garden, Kilkee, County Clare.

"Kilballyowen" Church ruins and graveyard near Cross, County Clare.

"Stone Interior Kilbaha" Public installation by Eddie Fennell, stonemason, Kilbaha, County Clare.

"Moyarta" Lynch Family vault in Moyarta Cemetery, Carrigaholt, County Clare.

"Piebalds at Feed" Three of the author's piebald donkeys.

"Thoor Ballylee" Tower home of W.B. Yeats near Gort, County Galway.

"O'Donohue's Heart, Fanore, The Burren." Sculpted wood grave marker of poet, philosopher, holy man, John O'Donohue buried in Creggagh Cemetery, The Burren, County Clare in January 2008.

"Winding Stairs" Thoor Ballylee near Gort, County Galway.

"Cliffs and Standing Stone" Atlantic coast south of Kilkee, County Clare.

"Madonna Moveen" Westward kitchen window of J.J. McMahon, farmer, Moveen, County Clare.

"Peninsula" West Clare from ten thousand feet taking off from Shannon for New York.

"Paraclete Moveen" The Moveen Lad (the author's champion donkey derby racer) in solitary confinement.

"Loaf and Bowl" The artist, Sean Lynch, photographed by his brother, Michael Lynch, with loaf and bowl.

Acknowledgments

The author wishes to thank the editors of the books and journals in which these poems first appeared, including POETRY IRELAND REVIEW, THE SOUTHERN REVIEW, CYPHERS (Dublin), THE POETRY REVIEW (UK), THE LONDON MAGAZINE, MUSE, and VIRGINIA QUARTERLY REVIEW.

"The Sin-eater," "Argyle in Agony," "Argyle's Vapors," and "Argyle's Balance" were collected in *Skating with Heather Grace*, Alfred A. Knopf, 1987, edited by Gordon Lish.

"Argyle's Ejaculations" and "Argyle's Retreat" were collected in *Grimalkin & Other Poems*, Jonathan Cape, 1994, edited by Robin Robertson.

"Argyle's Dream of the Churchdove," "Argyle in Carrigaholt," and "Argyle's Return to the Holy Island" were collected in *Still Life in Milford*, W.W. Norton & Co. (US) and Jonathan Cape (UK),1998, edited by Jill Bialosky and Robin Robertson.

"Argyle's Stone," "Argyle at Loop Head," "Argyle's Eucharist," and "A Corporal Work of Mercy" were collected in *Walking Papers*, W.W. Norton & Co. (US) and Jonathan Cape (UK), 2010, edited by Jill Bialosky and Robin Robertson.

"His Ambulations," "Argyle on Knocknagaroon," "He Posits Certain Mysteries," and "He Considers Not the Lilies but Their Excellencies" first appeared in POETRY.

"Argyle at the Ennis Friary," "Argyle Considers the Elements," and "His Repasts" first appeared in MICHIGAN QUARTERLY REVIEW.

"His Purgations," "He Weeps Among the Clare Antiquities," "Argyle Among the Moveen Lads," and "Recompense His Paraclete" first appeared in IMAGE: ART, FAITH AND MYSTERY.

Portions of the Introit first appeared in *The Christian Century*. Others were broadcast by BBC Radio III in a series of spoken-word essays entitled "The Feast of Language," Kate Bland, producer.

The author is likewise grateful to Michael and Sean Lynch whose images add immeasurably to this project, and to Lil Copan who first imagined such a book and brought it into being.

About the Author

Thomas Lynch is the author of four collections of poems, three books of essays and a book of stories, *Apparition & Late Fictions*. *The Undertaking* won the American Book Award and was a finalist for the National Book Award. His work has appeared in *The Atlantic* and *Granta, The New Yorker* and *Esquire, Poetry* and *The Paris Review,* also *The Times* (of New York, Los Angeles, London, and Ireland), and has been the subject of two documentary films, *Learning Gravity* by Cathal Black and PBS Frontline's *The Undertaking*. He lives in Milford, Michigan, and Moveen, West Clare.

About the Photographer

Michael Lynch is an avid traveler and photographer. He is a graduate of Wayne State University's Department of Mortuary Science and, like his father and grandfather, is a funeral director. He manages the Lynch & Sons Funeral Directors locations in Brighton and in Milford, Michigan, where he makes his home.

About the Artist

Sean Lynch is an artist and songwriter. His recorded work under the moniker 800Beloved includes, *Bouquet* (2008) and *Everything Purple* (2010). Before joining his father and brother in the family firm, he studied fine arts at the College of Creative Studies, Detroit. He lives and works in Milford, Michigan.

About Paraclete Press

Who We Are

Paraclete Press is a publisher of books, recordings, and DVDs on Christian spirituality. Our publishing represents a full expression of Christian belief and practice—from Catholic to Evangelical, from Protestant to Orthodox. We are the publishing arm of the Community of Jesus, an ecumenical monastic community in the Benedictine tradition. As such, we are uniquely positioned in the marketplace without connection to a large corporation and with informal relationships to many branches and denominations of faith.

What We Are Doing

BOOKS

Paraclete publishes books that show the richness and depth of what it means to be Christian. Although Benedictine spirituality is at the heart of all that we do, we publish books that reflect the Christian experience across many cultures, time periods, and houses of worship. We publish books that nourish the vibrant life of the church and its people—books about spiritual practice, formation, history, ideas, and customs.

We have several different series, including the best-selling Paraclete Essentials and Paraclete Giants series of classic texts in contemporary English; A Voice from the Monastery—men and women monastics writing about living a spiritual life today; award-winning literary faith fiction and poetry; and the Active Prayer Series that brings creativity and liveliness to any life of prayer.

RECORDINGS

From Gregorian chant to contemporary American choral works, our music recordings celebrate sacred choral music through the centuries. Paraclete distributes the recordings of the internationally acclaimed choir Gloriæ Dei Cantores, praised for their "rapt and fathomless spiritual intensity" by *American Record Guide*, and the Gloriæ Dei Cantores Schola, which specializes in the study and performance of Gregorian chant. Paraclete is also the exclusive North American distributor of the recordings of the Monastic Choir of St. Peter's Abbey in Solesmes, France, long considered to be a leading authority on Gregorian chant.

DVDS

Our DVDs offer spiritual help, healing, and biblical guidance for life issues: grief and loss, marriage, forgiveness, anger management, facing death, and spiritual formation.

Learn more about us at our website:
www.paracletepress.com, or call us toll-free at 1-800-451-5006.

More Important Poetry

FROM PARACLETE PRESS

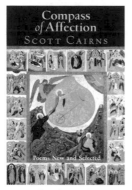

ISBN: 1-978-55725-503-7
$25, Hardcover, 148 pages

Compass of Affection
Scott Cairns

Scott Cairns expresses an immediate, incarnate theology of God's power and presence in the world. Spanning thirty years and including selections from four of his previous collections, *Compass of Affection* illuminates the poet's longstanding engagement with language as revelation, and with poetry as way of discovery.

"Scott Cairns is perhaps the most important and promising religious poet of his generation."
—*Prairie Schooner*

"The voice of Cairns is conversational and coaxing—confiding in us secrets that seem to be our own."
—*Publishers Weekly*

ISBN: 1-978-55725-599-0
$19, Trade paperback, 144 pages

Astonishments
Selected poems of Anna Kamieńska

EDITED AND TRANSLATED BY
Grażyna Drabik and David Curzon

Kamieńska's poems record the struggles of a rational mind with religious faith. Her spiritual quest has resulted in extraordinary poems on Job, other biblical personalities, and victims of the Holocaust. She explores the meaning of loss, grief, and human life. Her poetry expresses a fundamental gratitude for her own existence and that of other human beings as well as for myriad creatures, hedgehogs, birds, and "young leaves willing to open up to the sun."

Available from most booksellers or through Paraclete Press
www.paracletepress.com; 1-800-451-5006. Try your local bookstore first.